TRICKIEST!

19 SNEAKY ANIMALS

STEVE JENKINS

HOUGHTON MIFFLIN HARCOURT · BOSTON · NEW YORK

Trickiest!

Contents

Survival can be tricky.

For most animals, finding food and avoiding danger is a full-time job. A few of them survive by being bigger, stronger, or fiercer than other creatures. But many animals use tricks to catch their prey* or outsmart a predator. Some escape danger by pretending be a tree branch, a piece of seaweed, or a poisonous insect. Others startle their enemies with a flash of color or a sudden noise. Clever hunters fool their victims with disguises, lights, lures, or bubbles.

The animals in this book have come up with some surprising ways of staying alive.

* Words in blue can be found in the glossary on page 38.

Some animals have
tricky ways of catching
their prey.

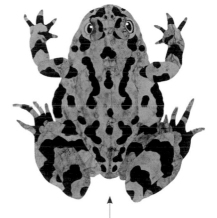

Other animals have
clever ways of staying
safe.

Crying wolf

The fork-tailed drongo cries in alarm if it spots a hawk or jackal. When other animals hear this cry, they stop what they are doing and rush for cover. But the drongo is tricky. Sometimes it warns of danger that is not really there. When a frightened animal drops a worm or other snack, the drongo swoops down and snatches it.

If the drongo uses its trick too often, other animals will ignore it. If this happens, the drongo fools them by imitating the warning calls of other creatures.

10 INCHES
(25 CENTIMETERS)

Where it lives
Central and
southern Africa

What it eats
Insects, small
animals

The drongo
can imitate the
calls of more
than 50 other
animals.

Living vine

The **green vine snake** looks like a tangled vine as it glides through the trees of the rain forest. With this disguise it can creep up on birds and other small animals. When the snake gets close enough, it strikes. It gives its victim a venomous bite, and then swallows it whole.

Where it lives
Central and South America

What it eats
Birds, rodents, frogs, lizards

The green vine snake's bite won't kill a human, but it is painful.

6½ FEET
(2 METERS)

Blowing bubbles

Humpback whales catch fish with a bubble net. They find a school of fish and swim in circles below it. As they swim, the whales blow out a constant stream of bubbles. The bubbles herd the fish into a tight ball. Then the whales take turns swimming straight through the ball of fish with their mouth wide open. They gulp down hundreds of fish at a time.

A humpback whale can eat as much as 3,000 pounds (1,362 kilograms) of food a day.

When a humpback whale smacks the water with its tail, fish are frightened and cluster together.

50 FEET
(15 METERS)

Where it lives
Oceans worldwide

What it eats
Fish, shrimp, krill

Casting shadows

The **reddish egret** wades through shallow water, spearing fish and frogs with its long beak. One of its tricks is to cast a shadow on the water by standing still and spreading its wings. Fish often seek shelter in shady places. When they gather in the shade of the egret's wings, the bird grabs them.

The reddish egret tosses a fish into the air and swallows it head first.

Where it lives
Southern United
States, Central
America, northern
South America

What it eats
Fish, frogs, crabs,
shrimp

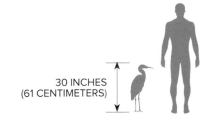

30 INCHES
(61 CENTIMETERS)

Fake worm

The **alligator snapping turtle** has an unusual way of catching fish. It rests on the bottom of a stream or pond. Then it opens its mouth and wiggles part of its tongue. This long red lure looks like a worm. When a curious fish comes near, the turtle grabs it.

Where it lives
Southeast United States

What it eats
Frogs, fish, snakes, birds, other turtles, dead animals

A snapping turtle can easily bite off a person's finger.

30 INCHES
(76 CENTIMETERS)

Deep-sea fishing

The **deep-sea hairy angler** lives in total darkness. Sprouting from its body are dozens of long filaments that can detect the motion of other animals in the water. The hairy angler dangles a lure—a glowing blue light on a long stalk. It eats the fish and shrimp that are attracted to its light.

Special bacteria produce the light in the hairy angler's lure.

The hairy angler can swallow a fish that is bigger than itself.

6 INCHES
(15 CENTIMETERS)

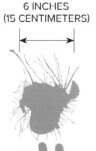

Where it lives
Atlantic, Pacific, and Indian Oceans

What it eats
Fish and shrimp

15

I can see you.

The **stoplight loosejaw** lives in the dark waters of the deep ocean. Most deep-sea creatures cannot see the color red. It appears black to them. But the stoplight loosejaw can see red. And it has a patch on its face that produces red light. So it can see the animals it preys upon, but they can't see it.

The stoplight loosejaw opens its mouth extra-wide to swallow large prey.

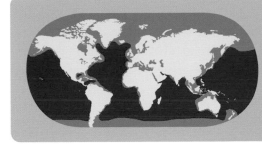

Where it lives
Deep oceans
worldwide

What it eats
Fish, shrimp,
krill

The glowing red spots
on this fish's face look
like a stoplight.

10 INCHES
(25 CENTIMETERS)

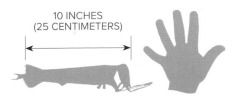

Ready, aim, fire!

The **archerfish** squirts a jet of water from its mouth to knock down insects. It can shoot down a moth or fly that is several feet away. It gulps down its prey the moment the insect hits the water.

Where it lives
India, New Guinea, northern Australia

What it eats
Insects

4 INCHES
(10 CENTIMETERS)

Don't touch!

Most people know that a wasp sting can be painful. Many birds know it too. The harmless **wasp beetle** has no stinger. But it looks like a real wasp, so birds and other predators avoid it.

Where it lives
Europe, Russia, Asia Minor

What it eats
Pollen, flower nectar

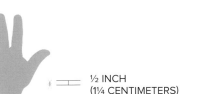

½ INCH
(1¼ CENTIMETERS)

This is a real wasp. It's not easy for a predator to tell the difference.

A silken snare

Unlike most spiders, the **bolas spider** does not build a web. It catches moths and other flying insects by casting a sticky silk thread. This spider attracts male moths by producing a chemical lure that smells like a female moth. When its prey gets close enough, the bolas spider snags it, reels it in, and eats it.

½ INCH
(1¼ CENTIMETERS)

Where it lives
The Americas,
Southeast Asia, Africa,
Australia

What it eats
Moths, flying insects

This spider is named after the bolas, a hunting weapon used by some South American native tribes. When thrown, the bolas wraps itself around the legs of a deer or other animal.

Pretty deadly

The **orchid mantis** looks like a delicate flower. But don't be fooled— this mantis is a fierce predator. It sits on a flower and waits quietly. When a flying insect gets close enough, the mantis grabs it with its spiky arms.

Where it lives
Southeast Asia

What it eats
Insects

2¾ INCHES
(7 CENTIMETERS)

The honeybee is one of the most common victims of an orchid mantis's ambush.

Living seaweed

Predators can easily mistake the **leafy sea dragon** for a piece of drifting seaweed. This relative of the seahorse hovers in the water and sucks up tiny animals with its long snout.

Where it lives
Coastal waters south of Australia

What it eats
Small shrimplike animals

The leafy sea dragon is actually a kind of fish.

9 INCHES
(23 CENTIMETERS)

Leafy lizard

The **satanic leaf-tailed gecko** makes its home in the trees of the rain forest. To hide itself, it grips a branch and sways gently in the breeze. Its tail even has holes and ragged edges that make it look like an old leaf.

Where it lives
Madagascar

What it eats
Insects

This gecko can also scare off a predator by opening its bright red mouth.

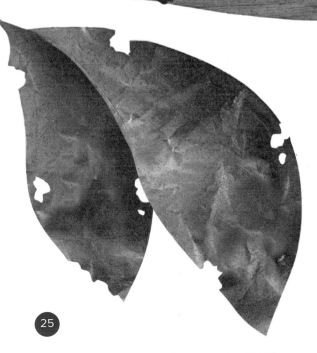

5 INCHES
(12½ CENTIMETERS)

Toad warning

Viewed from above, the **Oriental fire-bellied toad** blends in with green grass and leaves. But if it can't hide, the toad flips onto its back and displays its bright red belly. The toad's skin contains a deadly toxin, and the bright color warns attackers, "Don't eat me—I'm poisonous."

Where it lives
Korea, parts of China and Russia

What it eats
Worms, insects, spiders

The fire-bellied toad viewed from above.

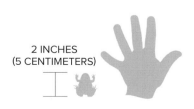

2 INCHES
(5 CENTIMETERS)

Click and glow

The **fire beetle** is a kind of click beetle. Click beetles roll onto their back and flip into the air to escape danger. The fire beetle is also bioluminescent— it produces its own light. It has two glowing spots on its back and one on its belly.

Where it lives
Southern United States, Central and South America

What it eats
Pollen, fruit, insects

This beetle's glowing spots are probably used to communicate with other fire beetles.

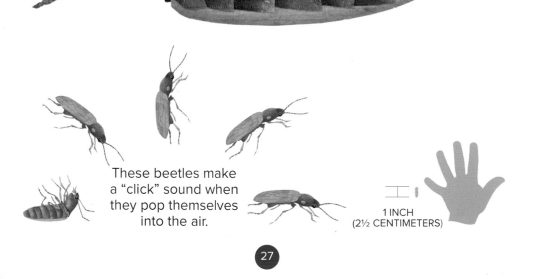

These beetles make a "click" sound when they pop themselves into the air.

1 INCH
(2½ CENTIMETERS)

27

Surprise!

Resting on a tree trunk with its wings folded, the **Io moth** blends in with the bark. When it is threatened, the moth spreads its wings and reveals two dark eyespots. These spots look like the eyes of a large animal, and their sudden appearance can frighten a predator.

The spines of the Io moth caterpillar contain a powerful venom. Touching or brushing against them results in a painful sting.

The adult Io moth doesn't eat anything— it has no mouth.

Where it lives
Eastern North America

What it eats
Caterpillars eat the leaves of trees and shrubs.

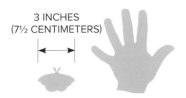

3 INCHES
(7½ CENTIMETERS)

It doesn't hurt.

The **blue-tailed skink** lives on an island in the Indian Ocean. Its colorful tail is meant to distract a predator. If it is attacked, the lizard can break off its tail and run away. After a while, the tail will grow back.

After the lizard's tail pops off, it wiggles and twitches. A hungry bird will go for the tail and the skink can escape.

Where it lives
Christmas Island

What it eats
Insects, spiders, worms

3 INCHES
(7½ CENTIMETERS)

Dark cloud

When danger threatens, the **giant Pacific octopus** ejects a cloud of black ink. Predators are confused and can't see the octopus as it makes its getaway.

15 FEET
(4½ METERS)

Octopuses can change their color and texture to match their surroundings.

Where it lives
Northern Pacific Ocean

What it eats
Shrimp, fish, clams

Playing dead

The **western hognose snake** has several ways of defending itself. If it is frightened, it makes a loud hissing noise. Next, it flattens its body, opens its mouth, and raises its head from the ground. This makes it look larger and more dangerous. But its best trick is "playing dead."

"Playing dead" is an good defense because many predators prefer to eat prey that they have killed themselves.

30 INCHES
(76 CENTIMETERS)

The hognose snake plays dead by rolling onto its back and lying motionless. It also sticks out its tongue and lets a little blood run from its mouth.

Where it lives
Central United States and Canada, Mexico

What it eats
Frogs, lizards, other snakes, birds, rodents

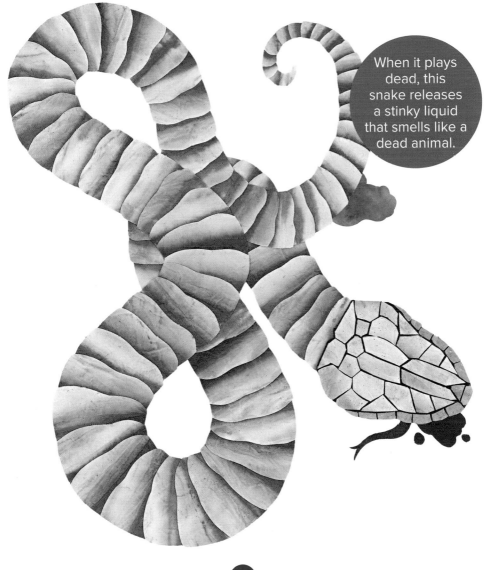

When it plays dead, this snake releases a stinky liquid that smells like a dead animal.

35

The animals on this page use tricks to help them catch and eat other animals.

reddish egret
page 12

archerfish
page 18

These animals have tricky ways of hunting.

humpback whale
page 10

bolas spider
page 20

stoplight loosejaw
page 16

drongo
page 6

These animals use imitation to catch their prey.

green vine snake
page 8

hairy angler
page 15

These animals use a lure to attract their victims.

orchid mantis
page 22

alligator snapping turtle
page 14

The animals on this page have clever ways of defending themselves.

firebellied toad
page 26

These animals warn, distract, or confuse their enemies.

blue-tailed skink
page 30

hognose snake
page 34

giant Pacific octopus
page 32

leaf-tailed gecko
page 24

These animals pretend to be something else.

wasp beetle
page 19

Io moth
page 28

leafy sea dragon
page 23

These animals startle an attacker.

fire beetle
page 27

Glossary

ambush
An attack made without warning, either from a hiding place or by an animal disguised as something harmless and unnoticed by its victim.

bacteria
Microscopic organisms that live almost everywhere on earth, including inside our bodies. Some bacteria cause illnesses, but others are helpful. The bacteria that live in the anglerfish's lure glow in the dark.

bioluminescent
Animals, plants, or bacteria that can produce their own light.

casting
Another word for throwing or tossing.

eyespot
A spot of color on an animal's body that looks like an eye. Eyespots can often startle and frighten away predators.

filaments
In sea creatures, long, thin growths or body parts. The anglerfish uses its filaments as sense organs that detect vibrations in the water.

hovers
Uses wings or fins to stay in one spot in the air (wasp beetle) or water (leafy sea dragon).

lure
A sight, sound, or smell that attracts an animal. Predators use lures—a body part, an odor, a light, or sound—to get their prey to come to them.

poisonous
In the animal world, a creature with poison in its skin or flesh. It must be handled or eaten to cause harm.

predator
An animal that eats other animals.

prey
An animal hunted and eaten by a predator.

toxin
A poison produced by a living organism.

venom
A poisonous fluid produced by animals as a predatory or defensive weapon.

venomous
In animals, a creature that injects venom with teeth, fangs, spines, or stingers.

Bibliography

The Animal Book. By Steve Jenkins. Houghton Mifflin, 2013.

Animal Life. By Heidi and Hans Jürgen Koch and Martin Rasper. H. F. Ullmann, 2008.

The Beetle Book. By Steve Jenkins. Houghton Mifflin, 2012.

Dramatic Displays. By Tim Knight. Heinemann Library, 2003.

The Encyclopedia of Mammals. Edited by David Macdonald. Brown Reference Group, 2006.

How Animals Work. By David Burnie. DK Publishing, 2010.

In the Deep Sea. By Sneed Collard III. Marshall Cavendish, 2006.

Life. By Martha Holmes and Michael Gunton. University of California Press, 2010.

The Life of Birds. By David Attenborough. Princeton University Press, 1998.

Natural World. By Amanda Wood and Mike Jolley. Wide Eyed Editions, 2016.

The Private Lives of Animals. By Roger Caras. Grosset and Dunlap, 1974.

For Robin

www.hmhco.com

The illustrations in this book were done in torn- and cut-paper collage.
The text type was set in Proxima Nova and New Century Schoolbook.
The display type was set in Geometric.

ISBN 978-0-544-93716-1 hardcover
ISBN 978-1-328-84195-7 paperback

Manufactured in China
SCP 10 9 8 7 6 5 4 3 2 1
4500661378

LEXILE: 880
F&P: R